TOY DESIGNER

TECHNOLOGY AND ENERGY

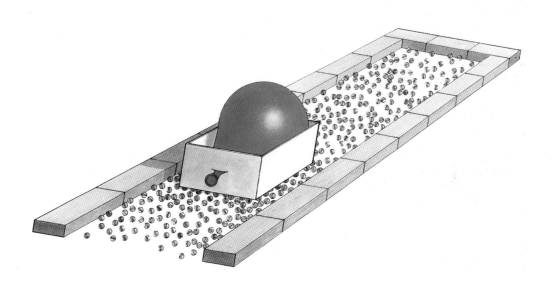

David Drew

Illustrated by Mike Gorman

RIGBY

CONTENTS

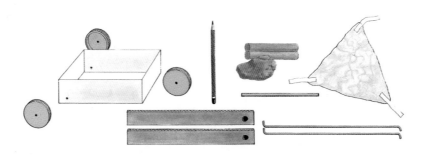

You Will Need These Items ...

Recycled Items

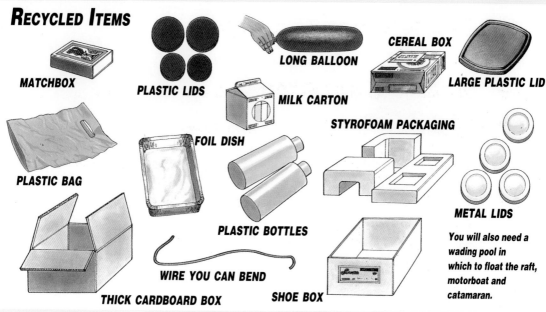

MATCHBOX

PLASTIC LIDS

LONG BALLOON

CEREAL BOX

LARGE PLASTIC LID

MILK CARTON

STYROFOAM PACKAGING

PLASTIC BAG

FOIL DISH

METAL LIDS

PLASTIC BOTTLES

You will also need a wading pool in which to float the raft, motorboat and catamaran.

WIRE YOU CAN BEND

THICK CARDBOARD BOX

SHOE BOX

Items From the Classroom

Items to Borrow From Home

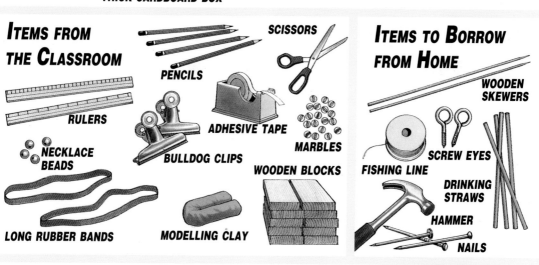

SCISSORS

PENCILS

WOODEN SKEWERS

RULERS

ADHESIVE TAPE

MARBLES

NECKLACE BEADS

BULLDOG CLIPS

WOODEN BLOCKS

SCREW EYES

FISHING LINE

DRINKING STRAWS

HAMMER

LONG RUBBER BANDS

MODELLING CLAY

NAILS

Items to Buy at a Hobby Shop

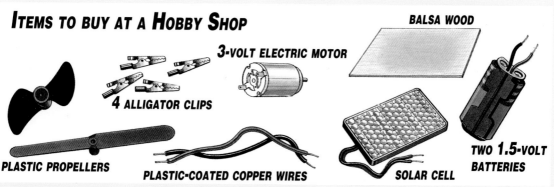

BALSA WOOD

3-VOLT ELECTRIC MOTOR

4 ALLIGATOR CLIPS

PLASTIC PROPELLERS

PLASTIC-COATED COPPER WIRES

SOLAR CELL

TWO 1.5-VOLT BATTERIES

Make a CABLECAR

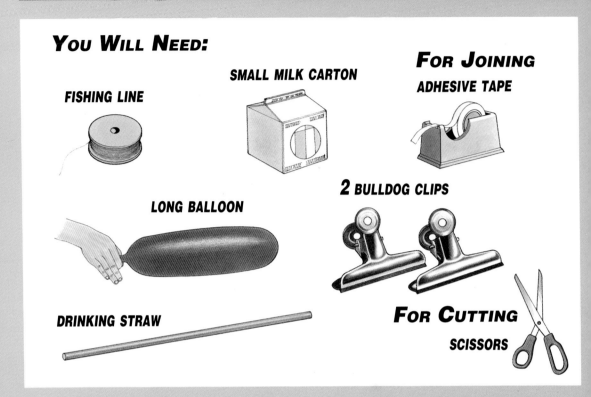

YOU WILL NEED:

FISHING LINE

SMALL MILK CARTON

FOR JOINING
ADHESIVE TAPE

LONG BALLOON

2 BULLDOG CLIPS

DRINKING STRAW

FOR CUTTING
SCISSORS

1. Blow up the balloon. Seal it with a bulldog clip.

2. Tape the straw and carton to the balloon.

3. Thread the fishing line through the straw.

4. Tie one end of the line to a tree.

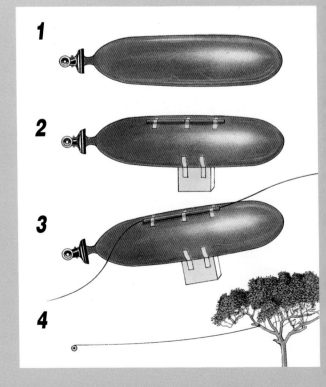

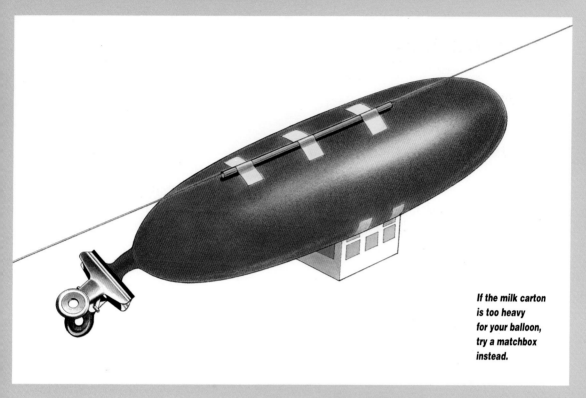

If the milk carton is too heavy for your balloon, try a matchbox instead.

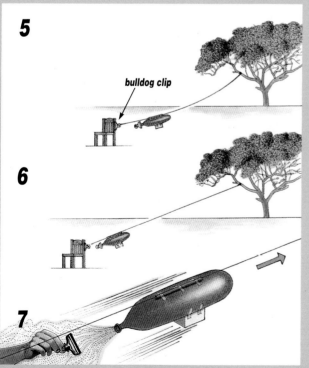

bulldog clip

5. Clip the other end to a chair.

6. The line must be tight: move the chair to tighten it.

7. Release the clip from the balloon. The balloon will be propelled up the line.

Make a RAFT

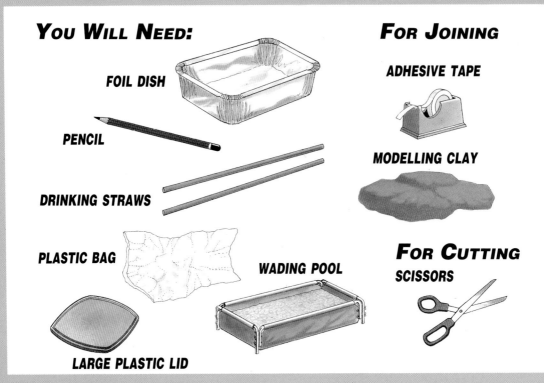

YOU WILL NEED:

FOIL DISH

PENCIL

DRINKING STRAWS

PLASTIC BAG

LARGE PLASTIC LID

WADING POOL

FOR JOINING

ADHESIVE TAPE

MODELLING CLAY

FOR CUTTING

SCISSORS

1. Join the pencil to the center of the foil dish with modelling clay.

2. Join the straws to the pencil with the tape.

3. Cut a square sail from the plastic bag.

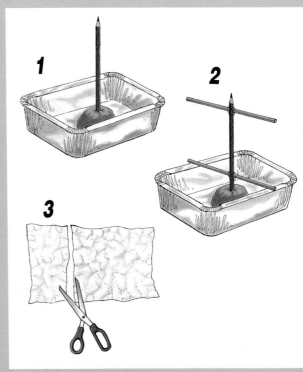

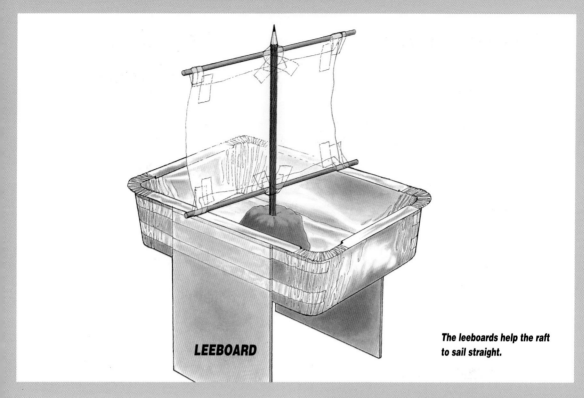

LEEBOARD

The leeboards help the raft to sail straight.

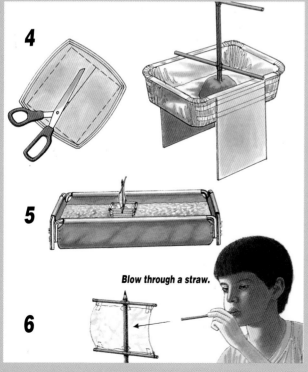

4

5

6

Blow through a straw.

4. Cut two leeboards from a large plastic lid. Tape one to each side of the raft.

5. Tape the sail to the straws. Put the raft in the water.

6. Blow on the sail to make the raft go.

Make a MOTORBOAT

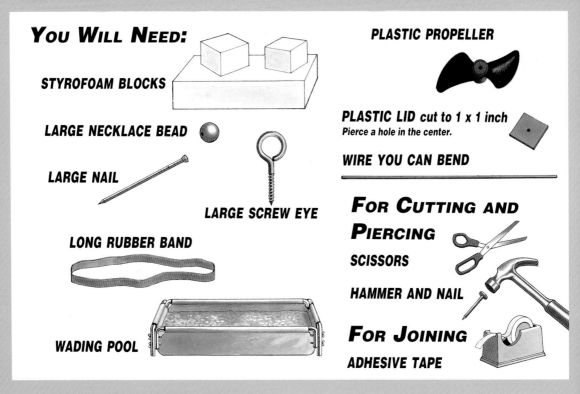

YOU WILL NEED:

STYROFOAM BLOCKS

LARGE NECKLACE BEAD

LARGE NAIL

LARGE SCREW EYE

LONG RUBBER BAND

WADING POOL

PLASTIC PROPELLER

PLASTIC LID cut to 1 x 1 inch
Pierce a hole in the center.

WIRE YOU CAN BEND

FOR CUTTING AND PIERCING
SCISSORS

HAMMER AND NAIL

FOR JOINING
ADHESIVE TAPE

1. Push the nail and the screw eye into the styrofoam block.
2. Bend the wire to make a hook, and pass it through the screw eye, plastic square, bead, and propeller.

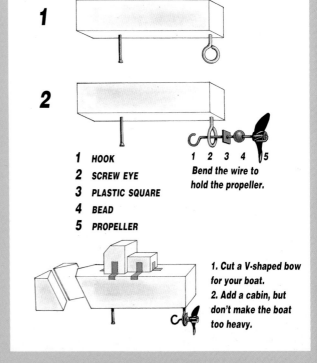

1
2

1 HOOK
2 SCREW EYE
3 PLASTIC SQUARE
4 BEAD
5 PROPELLER

1 2 3 4 5
Bend the wire to
hold the propeller.

1. Cut a V-shaped bow
for your boat.
2. Add a cabin, but
don't make the boat
too heavy.

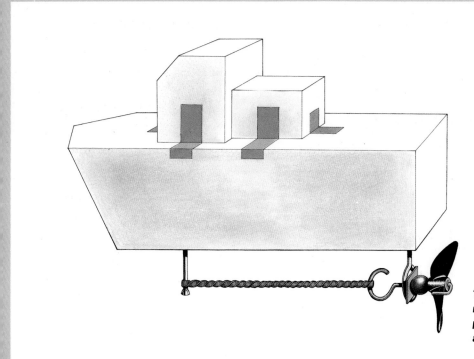

The energy in the rubber band will propel the boat about 12 inches.

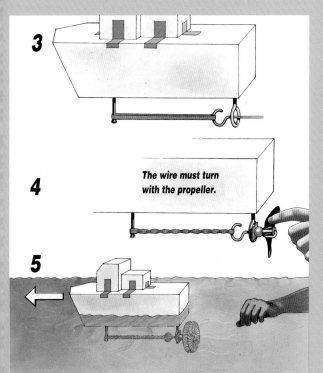

The wire must turn with the propeller.

3. Stretch the rubber band between the nail and the wire hook.

4. Turn the propeller to twist the rubber band.

5. Place the boat in the water and release the propeller.

Make a ROAD ROLLER

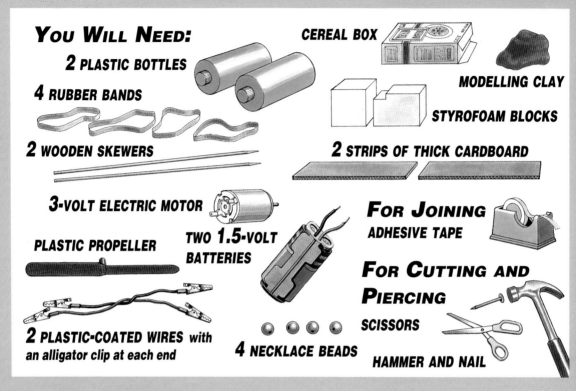

YOU WILL NEED:

2 PLASTIC BOTTLES

4 RUBBER BANDS

2 WOODEN SKEWERS

3-VOLT ELECTRIC MOTOR

PLASTIC PROPELLER

TWO **1.5**-VOLT BATTERIES

2 PLASTIC-COATED WIRES with an alligator clip at each end

4 NECKLACE BEADS

CEREAL BOX

MODELLING CLAY

STYROFOAM BLOCKS

2 STRIPS OF THICK CARDBOARD

FOR JOINING
ADHESIVE TAPE

FOR CUTTING AND PIERCING
SCISSORS
HAMMER AND NAIL

1. Make a hole in the center of each end of the two bottles.

2. Tape the cardboard strips to the box.

3. Pass the rubber bands around the bottles.

4. Place the bottles at each end of the box.

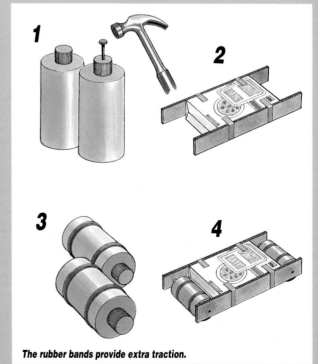

The rubber bands provide extra traction.

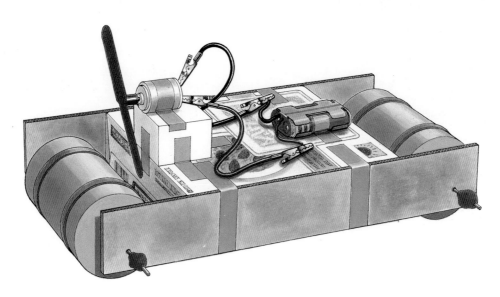

Place the road roller on a smooth floor. It will not move on carpet.

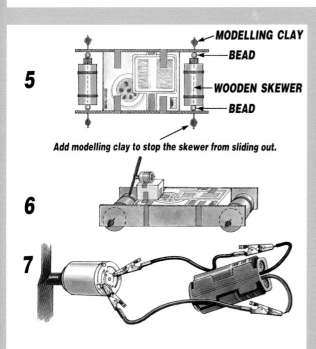

5

MODELLING CLAY

BEAD

WOODEN SKEWER

BEAD

Add modelling clay to stop the skewer from sliding out.

6

7

Attach the batteries to the motor with the wires like this.

5. Pass the skewers through the beads, cardboard, and bottles.
6. Tape a small block of styrofoam to one end of the box. Tape the motor on top. Attach the propeller to the motor.
7. Attach the wires and the motor will start.

Make a CATAMARAN

A catamaran is a boat with two hulls.

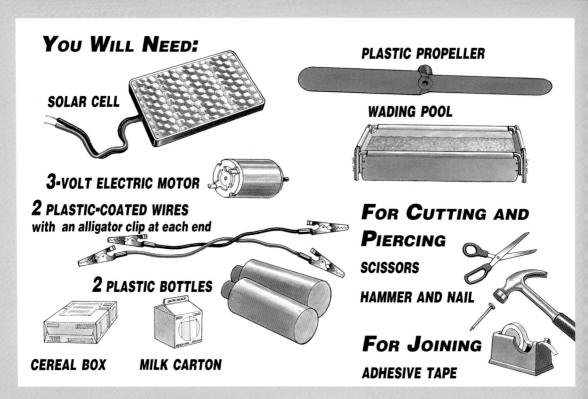

YOU WILL NEED:

SOLAR CELL

PLASTIC PROPELLER

WADING POOL

3-VOLT ELECTRIC MOTOR

2 PLASTIC-COATED WIRES with an alligator clip at each end

FOR CUTTING AND PIERCING
SCISSORS

HAMMER AND NAIL

2 PLASTIC BOTTLES

CEREAL BOX   **MILK CARTON**

FOR JOINING
ADHESIVE TAPE

1. Join the plastic bottles to the cereal box with the tape.
2. Screw the tops on to the bottles to keep the air inside.
3. Tape the milk carton to the top of the box, and tape the motor to the carton.

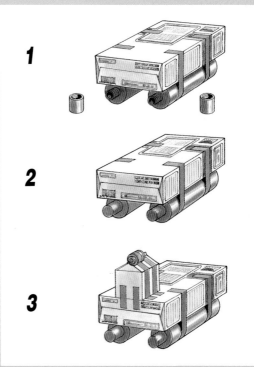

1

2

3

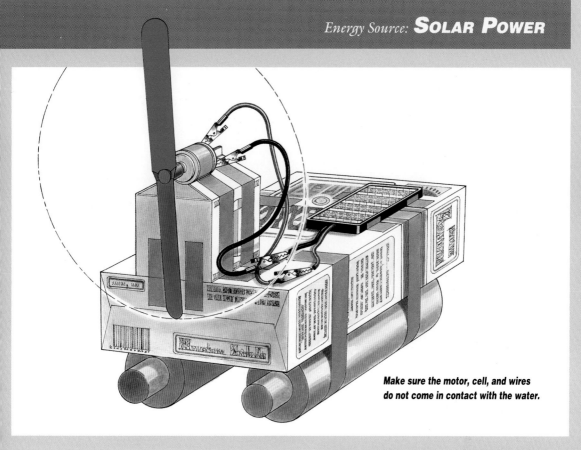

Make sure the motor, cell, and wires do not come in contact with the water.

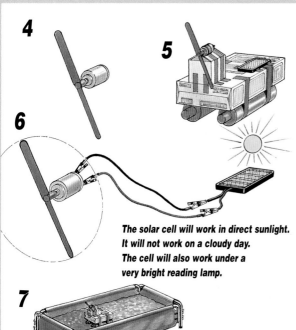

The solar cell will work in direct sunlight. It will not work on a cloudy day. The cell will also work under a very bright reading lamp.

4. Attach the propeller to the motor.
5. Tape the solar cell onto the catamaran.
6. Attach the wires, and the motor will turn the propeller.
7. Place the catamaran in the water.

Make a **JETMOBILE**

Energy Source: **JET PROPULSION**

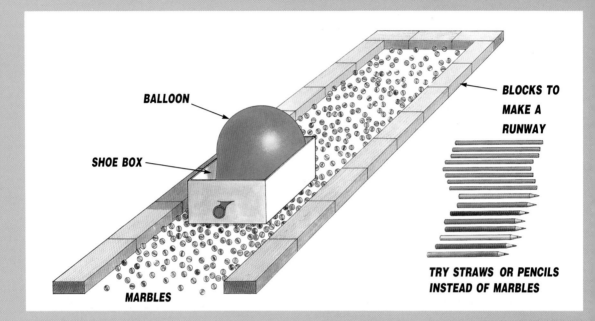

BALLOON

SHOE BOX

MARBLES

BLOCKS TO
MAKE A
RUNWAY

**TRY STRAWS OR PENCILS
INSTEAD OF MARBLES**

Make a **PADDLEBOAT**

Energy Source: **STORED ENERGY**

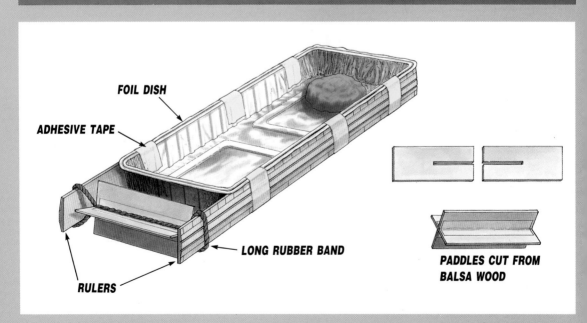

FOIL DISH

ADHESIVE TAPE

LONG RUBBER BAND

RULERS

**PADDLES CUT FROM
BALSA WOOD**

TOY DESIGNER

Only some of the items you will need
are shown here. What else will you need?
Write your own instructions.

Choose one of these projects.
Design it on paper, or make it.

A SAIL CAR WITH 3 WHEELS   *Energy Source:* **WIND POWER**

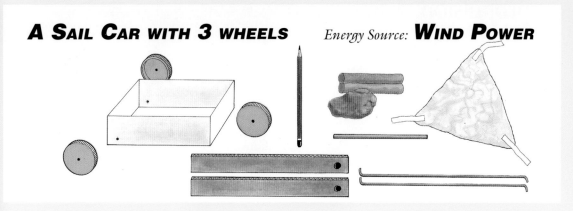

A ROAD TRAIN   *Energy Source:* **ELECTRICITY**

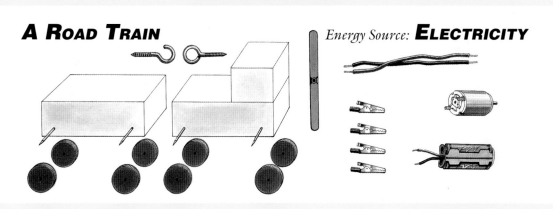

A TRIMARAN
**A trimaran is a boat
with three hulls.**

Energy Source: **JET PROPULSION**

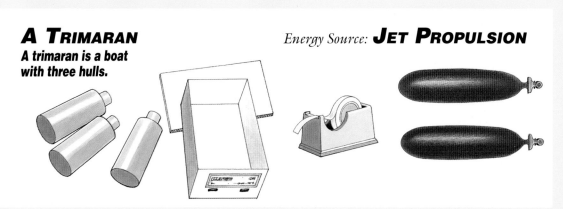

INDEX

HOBBY SUPPLIERS

Most or all of the "items to buy at a hobby shop" shown on page 3 can be purchased from the following addresses.

Australia

Educational Warehouse
528 Whitehorse Road
Surrey Hills, Victoria 3127
Phone   (03) 888 5511
Fax   (03) 836 8556

Canada

Exclusive Educational Products
243 Saunders Road
Barrie, Ontario L4M 6E7
Phone   (705) 725 1166
Fax   (705) 725 1167
Toll free   (800) 563 1166

United States

Science Kit and Boreal Laboratories
777 E. Park Drive
Tonawanda, NY 14150-6784
Toll free   (800) 828 7777

Frey Scientific
905 Hickory Lane
Mansfield, OH 44905
Toll free   (800) 225 3739